ice cream headache in my bone

phillippa yaa de villiers

ice cream

headache

in my

bone

poems

phillippa yaa de villiers

modjaji books

Publication © Modjaji Books 2017
Text © Phillippa Yaa de Villiers 2017
First published in 2017 by Modjaji Books
modjajibooks.co.za
ISBN 978-1-928215-32-5
Book, cover design and cover art: Megan Ross
Author photograph: Dean Hutton
Printed and bound by Digital Action SA

Set in Crimson Text

dedication

after the weeping the sleeping after the sleeping the ream

after the ream the perfection of living after perfection

after the rage an the reness

after the fire the green

to the memory of Lesley Joy Perkes

who once told me

she had an ice cream headache in her leg

and I knew exactly what she meant

Contents

Akoko nan
Leg of a hen

*The mother may step on her chicks
for protection or correction
never with the intention to kill*

what i found

when i was a child   life   was all around me
        it   chattered like a monkey and
sparkled – and sometimes stabbed softly
        like whispers
        like secrets that draw blood.
                i wanted to flow to the edge of the world and spill
                                                over, ride
                                        a tyre

                                down a swift river
        a l l   t h e   w a y   t o   t h e   s e a.

i wanted to grow   t

                            a

                            l

                            l

                            e

                            r   than the thick old pine tree

                                  i was only tall enough to climb

                                  when I hit thirteen –

i ate everything on my plate (good girl)

stared long at the long-limbed rainspider

with a scrambled egg mess on its black squat body,

            sprawled across her web woven between the timber stacked
behind

            daddy's workshop

      when

i went wandering

            in search of what i found

Apricot jam

when I was seven my mother told me

man ᐟarf nie auf ᐟer strasse essen

never eat in the street

you torment those who are starving. Her eyes

went monochrome on me, detached

to a five-year-old in Johannesburg's dusty streets,

1929:

eating a thick slice of her mother's

home-made white bread with apricot jam

and a black child asked her for some

and she refused, and when she grew up

haunted by her sin

she met a black child and said

you will never starve again,

you are mine;

she fed me thick slices of white bread with apricot jam

and the child tried to swallow

but the bread stuck in her throat.

The sweetness wouldn't come.

Hiatus

The first time I heard the word was after Daddy's double bypass.

He has a hiatus hernia, the whispers of the Big People:

        Daddy, my fortress. U n b u ilt by illness.

Hiatus   Mommy explains   is a gap, a hole,

an interruption in a continuum;

his organs are squeezing through

a small tear in his peritoneum.

I, at eleven imagine

organ   monkey   thoughts   roll   down

the stairs   he built smelling of cobra floorpolish

past the high window   he built morning light washing in.

He sits on the bed that   he made

in his new old flesh smelling of hospital

I hear his wheeze of breath

he pulls my reluctant hand, repulsed presses it

to an orange-sized lump at the top of his white belly.

That moment I knew

I would live longer than he –

Familiars

after Emily Dickinson

I
Red-lipped herald

My brother kept snakes. I wasn't too fond of

that narrow fellow in the grass

with an endless smile

and lovely spots,

t e r r i f i e d o f t h e m;

poison green boomslang

hanging like snot from the fever tree

on Uncle Bill's farm that holiday,

a week of nightmares.

They're more afraid of you than you are of them

don't be silly

and one sunny morning a darkbrown slither scattered us

kids fingerpainting on the lawn

and I wanting to be the hero grabbed the tail

a slash of redlips

fangs hooked into my hand:

I screamed with fear   I'm going to die

mother calmed: poor thing. It got a fright.

II
Egg eaters

Twenty-five and bronzed muscle my brother

was God. I wanted to make myself in his image

so I w h i n e d and begged and he gave me

a litter of egg-eaters, t o o t h l e s s he said, safe;

his large, nail-bitten hands placed them

carefully in a glass tank with soil and rocks,

pretty patterned bodies draped over a

twisted log like a display of trendy watch straps.

Then

they all escaped. After bathtime

I came back to a h i s s i n g room

friction of scales rasping against the carpet's texture,

black eyes glittering, forked tongues tasting the air.

I am not like you I said

and I don't even want to be.

Polite conversations

Is that your grandson, Bungy?

That colour looks so good on you with your skin

I wish I could tan as well as you

I always wished that I had curly hair

Such sensuous lips

Is that your son's girlfriend?

It really doesn't matter to me what colour you are

I am not a racist but

We blacks are not like that

While I was sleeping a forest of words grew up in my room. Fleshy stems forced through the carpet, succulents snaked up the walls and when I opened my eyes I could no longer see the door; the words took up all the air they theytheytheytheyhardened to trunks and divided themselves into leaves that became my bed and my pillow and the orange blanket that kept me warm, I could hardly see a thing never mind breathingand it was hot and stuffy and I don't know who left a panga under my pillow but next thing I was outside with a nice pile of dead wood to start a fire with.

Childhood maladies

Hallowe'en

is scaring and pretending and real life

when you're ten.

After June 1976 mommy took me on sabbatical with her:

trick or treating in

suburban Oak Park, Chicago;

scampering skeletons and ghosts and zombies,

light pierced the safety net of dark green trees,

wide immense streets,

and Tiffany's mom checked our loot because

kids' mouths got ripped to shreds

because razorblades planted in apples

by bad men,

because poison candy,

perverts.

i thrilled to the danger

her rage seething in

those big words

and

Mr Harris with an afro out to here

took me for Macdonalds

because he thought

i was a Soweto refugee

but i told him what i knew:

i'm not black, i declared

blacks are uncivilized

they will never rule our country

they need us whites.

i survived

tonsillitis and

shutup or I'll give you something to really cry about

children should be seen and not heard,

open wide:

the doctor's brittle

balsawood depressor

on my yellow tongue

and when i was fully grown

i wondered why

when i rang a stranger's doorbell

it felt like

sweets rained from the sky

like bombs in a world war two movie:

a childhood malady

wat nie doodmaak nie

maak vet.

The white room

We are from far

so far we don't even remember

when we were summoned

by some

internal message, or maybe

an invitation in the post –

and when I set off in my best body

someone else's name was on the envelope –

I was too far gone

already held in blue rubber hands

already covered in blood

already with a whole lot of people

to take care of.

The effort of living in skin

gasping and panting

hemmed in to a white cube,

burst out again, and again and again –

at six, at twenty, at thirty-four, at forty-two

each time insisting my body in,

or out, or elsewhere

from that w h i t e   room.

ice cream headache in my bone

adopted is odd is black is fabulous

homing

in to

awkward (as in) uncomfortable zones

the glitter in the dark

abandoned is even is white is fearful

balanced

but

bone is home

elastically animist

targeted billet-doux

droning alone

a family of songs

my vote is my secret

war burble in the enemy's throat

half-life

you forgot me

so hard that

my cells forgot to hold on to each other

bloodfleshbeing

a t o m i s e d

into a warm red mist

you absent-mindedly wipe away

as you walk through me

calling my name

annoyed

'cause you don't receive

a reply

i am in the landfill of your memory

like the jolly mess of persistent plastic

like radioactive waste

exuding its s l o w p o i s o n

With my whole heart

I

We need to get a black audience to read the scripts
make sure we're getting the messages right
said the client. I'm here, I ventured and she said
you don't count.

She's right I thought of course I don't count
ngoba angikhulumi
because I didn't grow up in a township/am not shut out by poverty/
or a language dammed in antiquity/purposely, relentlessly unseen/
I don't belong in a black demographic.

In a white demographic I don't belong.

Nor in a coloured demographic, do I belong.

I don't belong in demographics.

II

#occupycappuccino is not a revolution
but an opening volley of ironic intent;
because I'm preoccupied with connecting with whatever is meant
ngenhliziyo yami yonke
ngenhliziyo yami yonke

because I want fanon and shakespeare prescribed in schools
because my version of offshore investment is to buy into and consume
voraciously   responses to the colony and postcolony
to watch for flares shot up by incoherent night
to listen as complaining cracks open in songs
and write in bleeding letters you can read from the sky:

lady, what will it take for you to see I and I?

Strange fish

One summer night at a party, even booze

couldn't make the glinting chit chatting smooth

so rough I turned away

from the voices and the faces

and the light, threw off my shoes and the grass

speared the soft arches of my feet,

I unbuttoned the dress, unhooked the bra

and bent for a moment to feel my bodywarmth

diffuse from the clothes into the cooling earth;

watched by the stars

I offered myself to the river,

first toe then leg then all of me

crashed into the waiting water;

I plunged to the bottom and hung –

glimmering shadows danced away

hovered at the edge of the crocodile cave

like they didn't want to startle

this new strange fish.

Mmere Dane

Life – a dynamic dance through time.
Change is the only constant

Mouthfuls

At Singapore Zoo I ate breakfast with Ah
Meng, a 30-year-old orangutan, her gorgeous
red hair haloed by the golden sun, her brown
eyes bright at the tray of mangoes litchis
pineapples rambutans: a goddess sharing her
offering with me, her small hairless sibling.

I was an actress then, playing the black rhino
Thembalethu – our hope – in the production of
Horn of Sorrow, a victim murdered by a poacher's
bullet. As I sat, muscles stiff from carrying the
heavy horns of an animal identity, Ah Meng's black
jowls wobbled as she stuffed her cheek pouches,
filling the air with eloquent sucks and crunches,
mouthfuls of knowledge without words, her
body monstrous and gentle, the smell of her,

a forest of g r e e n s.

Flying north

In the flood plain of the dam the thorn trees prickle.

The sun, a flame thrower pointed at us, hazy mirage

people squinting. Silent.

The wind comes down, blowing south

and the trees shake their shoulders,

limbo dance under purple clouds

and a swallow   tries   to   fly   north,

and the wind blows it backwards

its wings flap,   frantic

thunder laughs, tumbled on its breath bird

                                    still tries to fly north

        on its b r e a t h   bird   bird   bird blown back

but that bird

that bird   still tries to fly

                still tries

                to fly

north.

Rapture in the dark

"Death came calling. Who ●oes not know his rasp of ree●s?" – *Wole Soyinka*

We have to keep going as if there is a future, but it's the end of the world,

the rapture, screaming bodies hurled to heaven, lost to hell; the callous

ticker tape of statistics burns holes in the sky

and the ritual murder of elephants and rhinos almost industrialised.

Our responses – automatic buttons pressed and autopilot setting

always looking west, and automatic opinions like/don't like

and the edge of the world subsides into flames. We will still do anything

to feel love and a cold airport voice instructs us to hurry to the boarding gate,

the ark is only half-built, the launch of the new strategy for the state

is waiting   for a coat of paint.

Here is life spread out in Eliot's etherised surgery,

       facing Soyinka's unwelcome guest,

like electricity failures: random, inconvenient, inevitable and pointless

to blame politicians. The world ended just a moment ago

for another rhino lying in its lonely blood. On the news an artist paints

the presidential naked penis – and we respond

with outrage.

Amputee

A man with an empty sleeve

reminds a woman of empty wombs, red tears,

residues of dreams.

She wants to ask him

even though his arm is no longer there

does it still itch?

On rainy days does it hurt?

How did it happen

and how are you now?

And she wishes he would ask her the same.

Can a child that was never born still laugh?

And when will it stop crying?

She imagines how painful it is for him,

ground zero, that blasted hole torn open

the invisible river of loss

the way that all the armfuls

of a tomorrow kind are gone –

amputee, woman

something missing

that only they can feel.

Guillotine

Luis wouldn't kiss me when I gave him that blow job

said he couldn't do that to his wife,

kisses were only for the woman he loves

says Bella.

That guy, hoots Gloria, he gave me a STD

my thing was so sore I could hardly walk,

he doesn't even know that she gave it to him.

What?

Ja, she's doing Fernando.

Luis's wife walks in at the door

hello ladies, the usual please.

Sure, madam, says Gloria, the basin is free

would you like to take a seat? Bella,

make the madam some tea.

Luis's wife lies back on the sink

her neck all open

like she's on the guillotine –

Headlines

Footsteps disappear in the formless mush behind the RDP flats,

where someone has hung a tyre in a mulberry tree,

remembering childhood.

Underfoot raw sewage bubbles out of pipes

dribbles down the narrow road and coats

the feet of passers-by like newspaper headlines

that refuse to be forgotten:

six-week-old baby raped;

two- and three-year-old toddlers

found murdered in toilet, and

Themba (meaning Hope), Nkosinathi (God is good) and

Thokozani (Rejoice)

blithely

stuff their mouths with bruise-coloured fruit,

take turns to swing.

They haven't yet learned to read.

Police line

Early morning –

the sun crosses a yellow police line,

Eleanor Street,

no questions asked of the huddle at the cops' feet,

a crumpled bleeding shivering woman

shot in the shoulder

on her way to work.

Rita runs out of her house

in her arms a blanket

she covers the victim

nobody is keeping her warm

nobody is taking care of her

nobody is helping

what is wrong with you?

Unsure what to do

the policemen, dull with sleep,

as Rita takes the woman's hand.

Secrets glimpsed between

after Sei Shōnagon

In a taxi a young man contorts his body to enter
the back seat: snug around his taut buttocks,
mickeymouse underpants prim below the belt.
The kous that binds the kinks under the clerk's
smooth hair wig. At prayer time, the mother
superior drinks hungrily from the milk bottle
behind the fridge door. Before the consultation
the doctor gasps into her palm and sniffs: checking
freshness of breath.

SweetBitter

The light weight of a four-year-old who fell
asleep while grocery shopping with father. A
woman leans heavily on my thigh as she pulls
herself on to the taxi seat – relief for her arthritic
knees.   The great-grandmother laughs at her
own naughty joke – a little girl in the dry husk
of a 93-year-old body. Hiding. On a warm Accra
morning coffin bearers dance to the busy music
of a brass band: the morning mist baked off the
glittering sea, the uncle inconsolable.

Tongue

English coul• be substitute• for French, Portuguese, Dutch, Man•arin or Spanish

The Lord said in my house there are many

mansions and it's true. My neighbour lives in Afrikaans

and the one on the other side is in Shangaan and I

live in the house of this poem. When we meet, me and my

neighbours, we meet in English, which we all

wear with our own styles. English is the market

and also the law like the time when Sister Mavis's druggie son

stole from me and was caught we heard the story

and the apology, there in the magistrate's court,

all wearing our best Englishes.

English forced us out of our own house of language:

burnt down the village, bombed the city.

Missionaries came after to dress our naked memories,

to recraft a path to God. The language that we own is the

English that they loaned, reworked to fit our mouths

our traditional attire and our fine tailored trousers:

smart and also hand me down.

For Corinna handing out hot dogs at the Sunday school barbecue,

her gold tooth glinting as she gives and gives, English is

a too tight dress that shows off too much and

Teacher Suzanne's English is too big and drags along the floor;

Andile's English is outside beating at the door.

From India to Aotearoa, from Kenya to St Kitts

English sits in our mouth like a new set of teeth –

not like the ones the dentist makes –

our English really fits because

we are native English speakers

and our English has been curried and spiced and tossed

into a nice salad with pineapple; we were torn apart from each other

and we want to go back home,

not back to where we were born-born

but back to a time when we were born in a tongue,

a tongue we can now use to find our tribe again.

Horse

You are whipped, subdued, beaten. Be strong, eat well,

grow. Agree to be saddled, endure the bit in your mouth,

bear the weight of him, of her, the boulders of their bums.

Behave well, do your best, go where the reins tell you to

tear up the earth with your hooves

hurry home, eat. At rest

flare your nostrils

savour the wood-smell, the drift of acacia pollen,

chilly breeze when the stable door opens

your tenderthinskin flexes, the crunch.

Bite if necessary, kick if you feel like it,

leap   over   fences

run   crazy   fast   as   you   can

change direction.

thenstop.

Do not help

your rider up.

The news

With a shock I realised

I am the people

they are talking about.

Don't mention the war

For C

Don't mention that your grandparents escaped gas ovens, think of something nice to say, anyway it was long ago and you're still here almost! Don't mention the men in balaclavas who beat you and your husband in front of your three-year-old child before locking you in the boot of your car. Crime brings down property values so don't mention it, don't mention Marikana and who gets what, and don't try to come up with a theory or make some claim about the relationship of crime to poverty, you've never been poor so make do with your lot and don't mention the robbers that crossed the double stand adventure garden and forced themselves into the French windows of your three-bedroomed farmhouse and dragged you out of your dream under the duck-down duvet. You pinched your lips together stifled sounds as they manhandled you around the house demanding money and kicked away the teacher's salary in your wallet because it was not enough. Don't mention that you looted your child's money box for the one hundred dollars that her aunt in the US sent to her in increments of ten dollars per birthday and Christmas for the past five years, don't mention them (especially to the child! She'll be FURIOUS). Don't mention that they tied you up and threatened to shoot you (Ag, there was no sign of a gun and they were young and sounded foreign) and don't mention that after they left you dragged yourself (and the chair you were tied to) to the panic button and pressed it with your chin and the security company took forty minutes to come and so you had ample time to think and mostly you thought

Wonderful! I am alive!

The mountain

(after the suici◦e of aparthei◦ operative Lotz)

Whilst doing the supper dishes: Kaya FM's breaking news

apartheid operative Lotz has shot himself. Asked for comment

Calata's son says he is saddened by the fact that now

they will never know exactly how their fathers died;

he enters my kitchen and sits down humbly, sorry for Lotz's

family but now we will never get that closure. He sighs.

Next morning four men smiling with conviction

shimmer through the decades on the internet. Goniwe,

Calata, Mkhonto, Mhlauli – fathers who never intended

to be ghosts. Husbands, brothers,

lovers – embraces still printed on the bodies that remain.

And the sister declares   I have not forgiven

and vultures lift from the carcass of reconciliation –

what breath, what wind, what relief

like when the sun breaks free of the mountain:

we accepted that Lotz

never apologised, never considered

the harm.

Akoma ntoso

Linked hearts
When you hear, see and feel me
and I do the same to you
an expression of solidarity

The baker's insomnia

(after Philipa Ju⋅as, worker)

Trying thoughts break into the soft house of sleep, splashing the white
walls with shadows. Noise. The body twists the sheets left, right. The mind
building, breaking, building, breaking. The pillow is a gagged hostage,
suffocating on secrets. The blanket discarded with a fretful kick. A hand
reaches for the Nokia phone: a tiny gleam, a hissed curse, the bedside light
clicks on. Piles of papers crowd each surface in the room, muttering threats,
repeating recipes. Alarm.

In the sink of night

dirty dishes wait, washed

by the light of the moon.

The prosecution rests

It was not rape, Your Honour:

it was not honour, your rape.

Your rape, honoured

not y o u.

Level minus three

Marble tiles reflect the leopard sky: blue spotted with

clouds. At Nelson Mandela Square

Ladies' lavatories

it is a woman's job to open the window every half hour.

She may not shit there; cleaners must ablute in the basement.

Every four hours she may take the service lift to level minus three,

follow the greenish grubby corridor to the lockers

holding bus tickets and street clothes and relief.

Back upstairs, a bespoke partition between two pairs

of feet; a flush, a wash, a flash of lipstick refreshed,

briefly their eyes meet –

then the customer flees.

Jakkals trou met wolf se vrou

For Ola Animashawun

When the old man gave up the I mean *his* ghost

the trees let go of leaves even though it was summer. And the

l e a v e s   f e l l   l i k e   *l i k e*

h a n d s   w a v i n g   g o o d b y e

a n d   t h e   r a i n

w a s   *f a l l i n g*   a n d   the   sun was shining

a n d   c h i l d r e n   d r e w   near

t h e   *w a l l s*   o f   t r i b u t e s   a n d   f l o w e r s ,

c a n d l e s   s   p   uttering little waxmesses

and the poor solace in doilied songs in ANC colours

vied for currency, blurred sympathy

of old rich liberals who wept for their son had left,

because the metaphor undressed was no more

he sank beneath your wis♦om like a stone

(in)finite, (im)mortal

and belonging to everyone,

and between the thick toes of grey barked trees

silent as elephants

we conducted our own ceremonies of grief –

fairy gardens tinkling with the wind chime sadness

of tiny shards of memory that lie in wait

to pierce an unconscious foot

days after the glass broke

the one you thought was forgotten

that pain sharp.

When I left home in search of something that would embrace me,

I mean all of me, it was forbidden

I mean embracing was I mean embracing me was I mean

I was forbidden just as equality was a communist plot;

I like Trevor Noah was born a crime

and Mandela reached long arms from his island

and picked me up and said

where did they hurt you I will donsa and shaya them

till they say uncle

lined in red an injury to one is an injury to all –

and a child holds all of time in her skip in her swing

always moving. The day Mandela died there was a moment

where the sun blazed through the raindrops

and there the wolf's wife with a veil on smiling

this is for ever darling, that pain in your sole, that blood on the floor

and all this r a i n a l l t h i s s u n l i g h t –

                                        now close your eyes and kiss the bride.

Mosi oa tunya

After Sharon by Aharon Shabtai

Running after words that disappear over edges like cataracts descending, the sound of water drowns out every other sound. It is all out of our hands, the authorities oppressors, the thrall of it, the thrill of it, running away from teargas grenades guns remembering memories from lived by others before us; decolonisation will always be a violent phenomenon, generational trauma wakes up in a new bed in a new body in a new skin, betrayal and violation taken like a man no, like a woman, no, like a strong black womxn, righteous and eternal martyr, a durable monument committed to the flames, indestructible, our destiny only that brings forth tears and rage and the smell of tyres on fire that brings forth tears and rage eternal like the durable monument of black womxn suffering, handled like a man, remembering, running away from teargas guns and grenades and generational trauma, the thrill of it, the thrall of it, it's all out of our hands, water drowns out every other sound, like cataracts descending, meaning disappears over edges, running.

Crush

in the time of #rhodesmustfall   #feesmustfall

spring falls over us   like a spell —

b r i e f ,   t a n t r u m   s h o w e r s   f a l l

j a c a r a n d a   b l o s s o m s   f a l l

in my restless garden smitten fruit trees bud restrained iris bursting to

weaver eggs in basket nests warm can barely wait the winter soil bored

for movement, everything wants

change;

and I go out of my way to watch you pick bouquets of music

arrange sound in faces coloured by your fantasy of freedom

intoxicated by your black eyes

I   s u r r e n d e r   common sense

to the sound of your stories and visions

like a falldown drunk in public middle-aged woman

shameless   e c s t a t i c grazed gash

broken mesh of pantyhose

a little blood, a little pain

I stand up and reach out again –

Freedom song

Under the Saturday morning sky

Kimberley Pride!

seven leggy drag queens stride by

in minis –

mince mince mince –

a baker's dozen of lesbians

bodyguards armoured in denim and leather

swagger swagger –

Kimberley Pride!

The whole procession sweating at 32 degrees

all smiling hard and wishing for a breeze

a massive rainbow flag like a parachute

overloaded taxis cars with queens in the boot

blonde wigs mascara boys and girls look sexy!

Red yellow green orange and what would you think

If the future was pink the future is pink

Take a ride on Kimberley Pride!

Past the big hole of disappointment — unafraid of disappointing past the church of disapproval — unafraid of disapproval

past the Russells and the Beares and the KFC

past the disses and the hisses and the terrified screams

grinning like a new bride, Kimberley Pride!

Tuelo teases Uncle, why you don't go

to the pageant, and watch those girls show

their pretty necks and legs and faces. Uncle says no.

That's not for me. We grew up different, you see.

That is not normal.

Normal?

Yes, normal. Like a man is a man, a woman is a woman…

Tuelo says, oh, I see.

You grew up with normal things like Non-European toilets, Bantu Education, thinking you were uncivilized, scared of being a play-white, relaxing your hair, litres of Lemon-lite, slegsblankes you can't sit here slegsblankes you can't enter, slegsblankes you're nothing more than ja baas nee baas, pass laws and perms

Tuelo grins: Aga shem

you didn't grow up with pride…

Definitely not with Kimberly Pride!

Odo nyera fie kwan

Love always finds its way home

Common wealth

I feel least sure of poems inspired by love, so let me write of other things.

The way your language speaks you

like an old man remembering a cherished child,

an ancient tongue which left its village as a baby and

formed new syllables around the foreign architecture of distant cities.

Home lies in your grandfather's eyes,

but the language that speaks you is your own.

You told me that you walked away from God. Your mother pleaded,

he gave you a job. The wages were terrible, but he sometimes let you

park the delivery van, that gave you your first taste of power. One evening

you were sweeping outside God's grocery store. On the opposite pavement

dreaded darkies came dancing, who painted the metropole

with their aerosol loneliness, and you dropped the broomstick

and the rules of your religion and the creeds of your community

and embraced them as brothers.

God got another young man to sweep out the shop, and

when you went in to buy condoms, he asked how your mother was;

frowning at the durex on the counter he asked

if you'd been home lately, and you said

I am home daddy, this is home for me,

this quick-hold-me-I'm-exploding-city,

this outpost of empire: Handsworth.

And we make home in music, our rebellion, in God Save the Queen,

this fascist regime, in redemption songs, now that we've found love

what are we gonna do with it

our common wealth: Reggae, Punk and Ska.

Oh, I don't know you, and I can't talk about love, we've only spent 96 hours

in the same room, so I'll talk about centuries

that cover the earth's crust like dust;

my young democracy is older than all the worlds that belong to you

speechless, as dumb as those endless photos you take

of sunsets and rock pools and the

sea. I don't know you,

I can only say what I like:

being beside the ocean with you,

your eyes a light house, your hips, the waves

tirelessly completing my expanding beach.

Cradle of humankind

This cave, cathedral with no register

of births. Australopithecus, Homo Erectus

and down the line, our ancestors lurch

across the shattered hills, the muted earth –

and the latest generation in hard hats

and boots, listens to the tour guide's prattle.

Like an affectionate hand on a child's head

the wind caresses the grass

and Heaven leans over to peer into human-ness -

its majesty, their looking glass;

like the sweet equality shared by lovers

each finds perfection housed in the other.

No miracle

My husband

I see the sun wake up in your eyes

each time she comes around, like

she is the earth and you busy

growing everything on it.

She's no miracle but

you take her apart like you're a mechanic

and she, the mayor's car

the mayor's mercedes benz,

hell no, his Bentley.

And the whole is more than the sum of its parts

like the shadow of a story

stretches far beyond the book,

and what am I but a reading lamp

standing silent by your shoulder

showing you what you want to see:

her lovely breasts, her pleated arse,

xhx! she just put on that body

in the cupboard of her mother's womb

and walked into the day, like me.

Foundation

When his wife finally told the truth that she didn't love him anymore,

and maybe she never had, the house stood up and walked away

with the pavement, concrete skirts swishing weirdly in the wind.

He alone in the cold gash in the ground, a worm exposed by the garden spade

white as a root and astonished. The shout froze in his mouth.

The knell   of steps   walking away   with his life,

waning like the moon, she stood on the stoep, weeping like a politician;

waved with one hand and with the other picked up

a fist-sized howling barking hairless red muscle,

wearing a gold collar and leash

and that's when he looked down;

realized the hole in his chest

raw as the one he was standing in.

He shouted and screamed as the house turned the corner

and moved on;

sobbing over and over

she took the dog as well

the bitch.

Erratic poetry

Erratic poems drop in unexpectedly, stroke

the side of the neck, bite the shoulder; relax the law

of clothing. The skin opens its thousand hands and takes the offering

somewhere a monk touches eternity in a morning dance

children space footsteps like sums building invisible worlds.

Erratic thoughts lightly hold your hand, they

disturb your deepsilences with throatsongs in

forgotten languages, a half-remembered scent, in

the moment of passion they call out a name you won't

recognise. In the morning you will wake

and find them gone. Don't be jealous, don't try to hold on.

They don't belong to anyone.

Elegy for jazz

I don't care how many babies

you abandoned on the way here, all your names

are just shoes you've grown out of, and what

you call family lies piled up behind you

and when you inhale you set them alight

and when you exhale

they burn.

Heroin dope and booze

and the telling of bitter truths

love pressed between pages

and names of the people

you never met who live inside you,

and pay their rent in the blues

yes they pay their rent in the blues –

and it was worth it for the sigh of your singing,

and in your voice the end of the world

and in your fingers the beginning of another

and you an ear listening

your bright eyes mirroring

the flames

False spring

I will not be deceived

by your warm air kisses and your breezy highs

your blue sky mornings with their runaway clouds

you won't tempt me to blossom outside

in the whip-crack cold of your winter pretender heart

Hartelus

Vir Pienaar, wie sy plaas gevin• het en met almal ge•eel

We turn off the main road past Tonteldoos and Hartelus to Stofberg, a sulky yellow horned moon on the left hand side. Window down on the warm evening, a vlei full of frogs that sounds like something I once read about — New Year's Day in a shanty town where all the women come out beating their buckets with wooden spoons and it's so loud we almost hallucinate, turn to each other with deaf grins —

and the grass sings a wild quiet melody to itself, behind us day pulls up a violet blanket with a vermilion sigh —

flying ants rise on paper wings:

a million

d e l i c a t e wishes.

Bones

All she knows is what she remembers:

her mind field   a kraal of sanity with a barrier of thorns

to keep her safely in.

In the cracked triangle of mirror she searches her face

opening the drawers of eyes, lifting the soft texture of cheek

and chin to find what was left within; memories are

buried in her flesh like bones.

She cannot see them now.

While she sleeps her skeleton stands up and paints her life,

the hand covers the blackboard with poetry, stories

roam through the pages of her students;

love waits at the door ready to carry her books home

and children, eager for life

burst out of her womb

and run to the laughing river.

Her son is a stranger who comes on Sundays.

After lunch, he takes her for a walk. The way he walks

reminds her of   someone.

The silence between them is littered with bones.

Doorbell

One day finally she goes out just to see someone

leaves the old house – pressed ceilings, generous rooms

infused memories of first steps, first words, last rites;

her mate deceased, her children emigrated

the garden cluttered and overgrown. Squeezed into

that blue paisley dress, no makeup and her hair a mess

in the cold white light of the shopping mall

a young man brownmuscle and crispshirt

selling beauty products from the Dead Sea, says

they will make her young again. She tells him how she slept

on the beach in a ruined Baha'i temple near Akko and how she missed

the trip to the Dead Sea, exploring the shuk with a lover

there just isn't enough time to do everything. She asks him if

he plans to travel, he laughs and shrugs

if I could go with someone like you.

Under the sun the roof tiles expand

after years of no visitors

the doorbell rings.

Unsung

for Xiancheng Hu, Xiao Kaiyu, Isabel Aguirre an⋅ Zhou Weichi

The Great Wall of China, they see it from the moon.

When the world collapses into dust or fire

we will remember the firewall that kept Chinese curiosity

tethered to its own monsoon history, silenced twitter,

only one face on the mind's book: the ancient one

impassive and solid. Walls protect and also restrain:

pain mortars the brick of fear, can love make a wall fall?

Friendship is a walk along an endless silence,

memory uncaptured like birds. From the moon

I can see us on opposite sides of the wall, our conversation

a song that can never be

unsung.

coming to grips with Chinese

ying

characters grow in silence

and out of silence

sharpen themselves

pierce the page

o v e r t h r o w

the tyranny

of

w h i t e

yang

for poetry to exist

characters have to break free

of the page claiming voices

writing themselves on the ear

on the air on this moment

we call infinity

Cleansing element

Colossus statuesque white bulges against a cobalt sky.

Monumental cumulus c r o w d the eye.

A phalanx of galleons crowned with cannons cocked d i s p e r s e s.

dragons rear and rage, claws poised c o l l a p s e to   f l u f f.

stallions canter their silh o u e t   t   e   s   to silken s h r e ds —

nimble filigree

ineffable

psychosis of the weather —

heat from sweating trees, the swelter outside the shade.

Roiling vapours darken to grey, thicken to purple, press out the sun.

heavy vessels collideexplode

flash, attack, thundercrash, multitudes hurled to earth,

    r u s h   h o u r   r a i n   p u l s i n g

    s l e e k   b l a c k   s t r e e t s —

remnants of the storm:

insistent river, plastic bag tacking

the new-born breeze.

Road music

There's a party on the radio, fat yellow horns barge

through rhythms ...

rhythms piled like empty cardboxes

horns knock them down then run around

build them up again, and the sun runs aground

as we take the highway south, the Corolla falls into

the land's black and toothless mouth, we four friends

on an adventure, hooting and lagging at the racists glaring

at the Wimpy this side of Bloemfontein. We're Fela-feisty,

having fun extra loud for everyone's benefit; in the toilets

the china gleams immaculate from her endless

vryf, a slight woman waits beside a plastic plate

brown cents discarded by the tight-arsed class,

heavy with our freedom beating her wings a-quiver

under the blue overall. The blond petrol jockey

hides his smile while his

sourpuss uncle sulks over our money and

we turn up the sound and make an extra round of the pumps

a bunch of hell-bent commies fist-punching and laughing,

shrieking there'll be sorrow tears and blood

and we're gone out on the road again, headlights writing

graffiti on the wall of the platteland night

and there's a hearse in the slow lane

shark without an appetite

single candle burning steady on the still coffin

two men side by side on the front seat

everyone at peace

and as we overtake

we fall

silent

into the immense music

of the turning sky.

like jesus

i wish like jesus i could swan

across westdene dam in my purewhite tekkies

to tell you things like i am a miracle waiting to
happen

if only you believed -

i want to tell you

stand up and walk, walk away from that

skorokoro wheelchair that they donated

'cos they don't need it since oubaas died

you, you also don't need it

walk away from that man who strangles your neck

with his pet hungry python, walk away

because you can. i believe in you

and when you've broken free, you will run

your gladdening footsteps will stomp the red ants,

trample the disappointment to sommer sault up

lighter and lighter

new rain on a dry pavement

walking like jesus on a land

that is changing all the time

into something we can drink

Repeat after me

Life is a language lesson. The child discovers

what I am called is not who I am.

A name is a fence around a field of

nodding concepts   wildflowers birds and bees –

ego system easy come easy go   back where you belong voetsek

What is black? To become   one has to first

be.

I create a shape that then starts to fall apart

a continent with a bulge, a horn and a cape

theatrical - a brown l a n d am I

lazing under clouds, drinking deep sips of the sky

in a daze   grassroots digging in   to   me

what is black? To become   one first has to

be.

B e c o m i n g   an earthquake   shatters the horizon

a fortress   collapses into the sea

an explorer   discovers

a decaying trunk filled with scrolls

that disintegrate as they come to light:

i am excavating my frozen tongue   a mummified Neanderthal

intimate   civilizations   roam   uncharted territory

what is black? To become   one

first has   to be.

Author's Note

These poems have been created over the past seven years. This book could not have come into existence without the generosity of many people and institutions. The University of the Witwatersrand provided a generous subvention towards the production of this book. Many of the poems were composed during a Masters in Creative Writing, thanks to Lancaster University for the Overseas Scholarship. With gratitude to my tutor Brian McCabe, the other teachers on the programme and the cohort 2012-2014.

Some of the poems have appeared in print elsewhere, in different forms and sometimes with different titles:

- "Common Wealth" in *POUi: Cave Hill Journal of Creative Writing*, No 9
- "Bones", "Don't Mention The War", "Freedom Song" and "Amputee" were in the publication of the *Berlin Poesiefestival* (2012) and *Ankunft eines weiteren Tages* (2013)
- "Rapture in the dark" and "Mouthfuls" in *For Rhino in a Shrinking World* (2013)
- "Tongue" in the *Bridgewater International Poetry Festival* (2013)
- "Guillotine" in *Plume* (Dec 2014)
- "Police Line" and "Horse" in *New Coin* no 51 (June 2016)
- "With my whole heart" in *scrutiny 2* issue 21.1(2016)
- "Elegy for Jazz" in *To Breathe into Another Voice: A South African Anthology of Jazz Poetry* (2017)
- "Road Music" and "like jesus" will appear in *Illuminations Journal* (Sept 2017)
- "half-life" in *Atlanta Review* (Spring 2018)
- "The baker's insomnia" has been awarded an Honourable Mention in the Genjuan International Haibun Contest (2017).

I thank my publisher Colleen Higgs, who has brought my words to print since 2006, and the extraordinary Gabeba Baderoon, who gently brought the shimmer out of the poems, and woke many sleepers. Vangi Gantsho, Robert Muponde, Raphael D'Abdon, Bronwyn Law-Viljoen, Pamela Nichols, Mphutlane wa Bofelo, Tshifhiwa Mukwevho and Pervaiz Khan who read this manuscript and gave comments and feedback. My son Felix and family and friends, particularly Myesha Jenkins and Makhosazana Xaba, who all celebrate my success and commiserate my failures - I can't do without you - thank you.

I would also like to thank the poets of Jozi House of Poetry, the IKS South African Poetry Project (ZAPP), friends and associates who allowed me to write parts of their stories, artists and musicians associated with the Afrikan Freedom Station and Roots Grown Deep, the creative families.

asymptote

perfection

life

you

we have done

our best to do justice

to that muse

amused

Acknowledgements

Music and sound influenced these poems - Jennifer Ferguson's lyric Suburban Hum inspired the line 'life was all around me' in "what I found". In "Jakkals trou met wolf se vrou" Leonard Cohen's 'he sank beneath your wisdom like a stone' wrote itself in, a mirror. The sound of chants and freedom songs, particularly during #feesmustfall demonstrations, added to a Kgositsile sensibility that affected many poems, especially "Jakkals trou met wolf se vrou" and "Mosi oa tunya".

Printed in the United States
By Bookmasters